Pebble® Bilingüe/Bilingual Plus

¿QUÉ HAY EN MiPlato?

FRUTAS en MiPlato

WHAT'S ON MyPlate?

FRUITS on MyPlate

por/by Mari Schuh

Editora consultora/Consulting Editor:
Gail Saunders-Smith, PhD

Consultora/Consultant: Barbara J. Rolls, PhD
Guthrie Chair en Nutrición/Guthrie Chair in Nutrition
Pennsylvania State University
University Park, Pennsylvania

CAPSTONE PRESS
a capstone imprint

Pebble Plus is published by Capstone Press,
1710 Roe Crest Drive, North Mankato, Minnesota 56003
www.capstonepub.com

Library of Congress Cataloging-in-Publication Data
Schuh, Mari C., 1975–
  Frutas en miplato = Fruits on myplate / por Mari Schuh ; editora consultora, Gail Saunders-Smith, PhD.
    pages cm. — (Pebble plus bilingüe. ¿Qué hay en miplato? = Pebble plus bilingual. What's on myplate?)
  Spanish and English.
  Audience: K to grade 3
  Includes index.
  ISBN 978-1-62065-942-7 (library binding)
  ISBN 978-1-4765-1753-7 (ebook PDF)
1. Fruit—Juvenile literature. I. Saunders-Smith, Gail, editor. II. Schuh, Mari C., 1975– Fruits on myplate. Spanish.
III. Schuh, Mari C., 1975– Fruits on myplate. IV. Title. V. Title: Fruits on myplate. VI. Title: Frutas en miplato.
VII. Title: Fruits on myplate.
  SB357.2.S3818 2013
  634—dc23   2012022650

Summary: Simple text and photos describe USDA's MyPlate tool and healthy fruit choices for children—in both
English and Spanish

Editorial Credits
Jeni Wittrock, editor; Strictly Spanish, translation services; Sarah Bennett, designer; Eric Manske, bilingual book
designer; Svetlana Zhurkin, media researcher; Jennifer Walker, production specialist; Sarah Schuette, photo stylist;
Marcy Morin, studio scheduler

Photo Credits
All photos by Capstone Studio/Karon Dubke except:
Shutterstock: brulove, cover (left), LeventeGyori, cover (right), Pinkcandy, back cover; USDA, cover (inset), 5

The author dedicates this book to Eat Right Racine's Heidi Fannin, who
is more passionate about healthy eating than anyone the author knows.

Information in this book supports
the U.S. Department of Agriculture's
MyPlate food guidance system found at
www.choosemyplate.gov. Food amounts
listed in this book are based on daily
recommendations for children ages 4-8.
The amounts listed in this book are
appropriate for children who get less than
30 minutes a day of moderate physical
activity, beyond normal daily activities.
Children who are more physically active
may be able to eat more while staying
within calorie needs. The U.S. Department
of Agriculture (USDA) does not endorse
any products, services, or organizations.

Note to Parents and Teachers

The ¿Qué hay en MiPlato?/What's on MyPlate? series supports national science standards
related to health and nutrition. This book describes and illustrates MyPlate's fruit
recommendations. The images support early readers in understanding the text. The repetition of
words and phrases helps early readers learn new words. This book also introduces early readers
to subject-specific vocabulary words, which are defined in the Glossary section. Early readers
may need assistance to read some words and to use the Table of Contents, Glossary, Internet
Sites, and Index sections of the book.

Printed in China.
092012   006934LEOS13

Table of Contents

Tabla de contenidos

MyPlate/ MiPlato

Fruits are a sweet part of MyPlate.
MyPlate is a tool that
helps you eat healthy food.

Las frutas son una parte dulce de MiPlato.
MiPlato es una herramienta que te
ayuda a comer alimentos saludables.

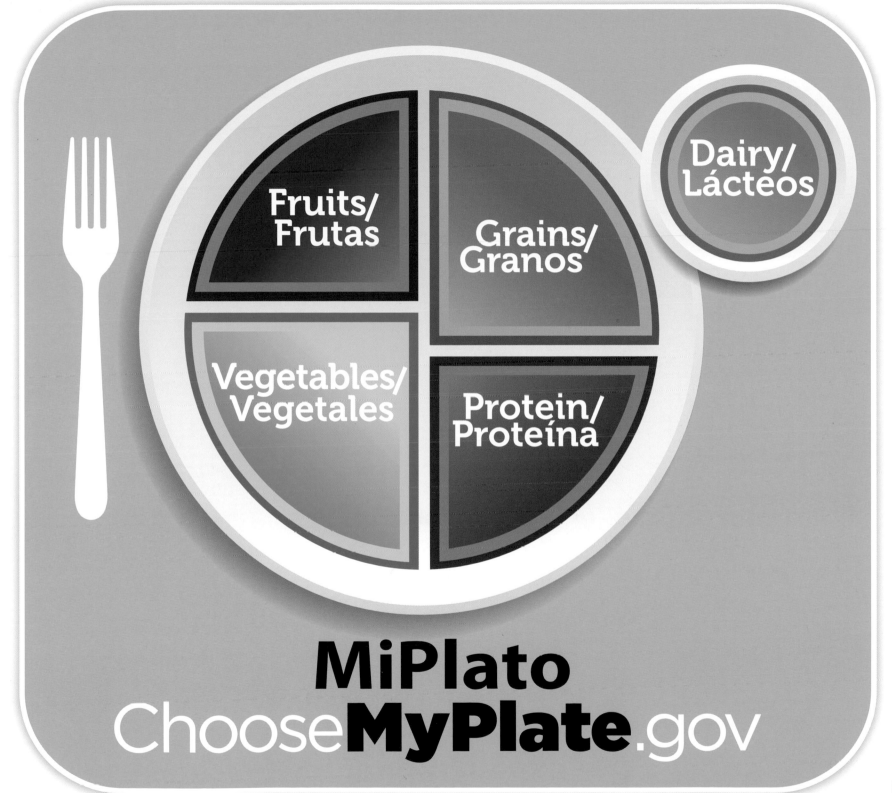

MiPlato
ChooseMyPlate.gov

A healthy meal
fills half your plate
with fruits and vegetables.

Una comida saludable llena
la mitad de tu plato
con frutas y vegetales.

6

Kids should eat about 1½ cups (360 milliliters) of fruit every day.

Los niños deberían comer alrededor de 1½ tazas (360 mililitros) de fruta cada día.

All Kinds of Fruit/
Todo tipo de frutas

Have you seen fruit growing?

Fruit grows on trees, bushes, and vines.

Fruits have seeds.

¿Has visto una fruta crecer?

Las frutas crecen en árboles,

arbustos y parras.

Las frutas tienen semillas.

10

You can eat fruit in many ways.

Fruit can be fresh,

dried, canned, or frozen.

Puedes comer fruta de muchas maneras.

La fruta puede ser fresca, seca,

enlatada o congelada.

Eat the colors of the rainbow.
Munch on pineapples, bananas,
grapes, and berries.

Come los colores del arcoíris.
Disfruta piñas, bananas,
uvas y fresas.

Fruit comes in
many shapes and sizes.
Try a new fruit
for lunch.

Las frutas vienen de muchas
formas y tamaños.
Prueba una nueva fruta
para el almuerzo.

Fruit makes a great snack.

Share some fruit with a friend.

_____

La fruta es una gran merienda.

Comparte fruta con un amigo.

How Much to Eat/
Cuánto comer

Kids need to eat three servings of fruit every day. That's about 1½ cups of fruit. To get 1½ cups, pick three servings of your favorite fruits.

Los niños necesitan comer tres porciones de fruta todos los días. Eso es más o menos 1½ tazas de fruta. Para comer 1½ tazas, selecciona tres porciones de tus frutas favoritas.

½ cup (120 mL) pineapple chunks

½ taza (120 ml) de trozos de piña

½ cup (120 mL) grapes

½ taza (120 ml) de uvas

¼ cup (60 mL) dried fruit

¼ taza (60 ml) de fruta seca

1 small orange

1 naranja pequeña

1 small banana

1 banana pequeña

½ cup (120 mL) 100-percent fruit juice

½ taza (120 ml) de 100 por ciento jugo de frutas

½ cup (120 mL) applesauce
(single serving container)

½ taza (120 ml) de compota de manzana (envase de una porción)

½ cup (120 mL) halved strawberries

½ taza (120 ml) de fresas a la mitad

Glossary

canned—sealed in a container to last longer; canned fruit that is packed in water or juice is healthier than canned fruit in syrup

dried—having most of the water taken out; people often eat dried peaches, apples, pears, plums, and figs

fruit—the fleshy, juicy part of a plant; fruit has seeds

MyPlate—a food plan that reminds people to eat healthful food and be active; MyPlate was created by the U.S. Department of Agriculture

serving—one helping of food

snack—a small amount of food people eat between meals

Internet Sites

FactHound offers a safe, fun way to find Internet sites related to this book. All of the sites on FactHound have been researched by our staff.

Here's all you do:

Visit *www.facthound.com*

Type in this code: 9781620659427

Super-cool stuff! Check out projects, games and lots more at **www.capstonekids.com**

Glosario

enlatada—sellada en un recipiente para que dure más; fruta enlatada en agua o jugo es más saludable que la fruta enlatada en sirope

la fruta—la parte jugosa y carnosa de una planta; la fruta tiene semillas

la merienda—una pequeña cantidad de alimentos que la gente come entre comidas

MiPlato—un plan de alimentos que hace recordar a la gente de comer alimentos saludables y de estar activos; MiPlato fue creado por el Departamento de Agricultura de EE.UU.

la porción—una ración de alimento

seca—que se le sacó la mayor cantidad de agua; las personas con frecuencia comen duraznos, manzanas, peras, ciruelas e higos secos

Sitios de Internet

FactHound brinda una forma segura y divertida de encontrar sitios de Internet relacionados con este libro. Todos los sitios en FactHound han sido investigados por nuestro personal.

Esto es todo lo que tienes que hacer:

Visita: *www.facthound.com*

Ingresa este código: 9781620659427

Index

Índice